Kwame Mintah

Pick Her Flowers

ISBN (Paperback): 978-1-916849-56-3

ISBN (Hardback): 978-1-916849-57-0

Cover Design by Woodbridge Publishers and Jalen Whitner.

WOODBRIDGE
PUBLISHERS

To my mother, Alberta,
Sister, Nyama, and Aunty Rachel.

I quite literally would not be here without the three
of you in my corner. My gratitude is immeasurable.
You are at the core of my drive to change our lives
through my art.

Table of Contents

Foreword by
Dhayana Alejandrina

In the heart of Kwame Mintah's verses lies a journey etched with hardship and resilience. Born amidst Liberia's civil war, separated from his parents, he found refuge in poetry—a divine calling. From the refugee camp to the streets of Philadelphia, Kwame's spirit refused surrender. His words, a reflection of inner strength, resonate with the authenticity forged in adversity.

Through verses, Kwame carries a vision—a vision to open doors for emerging artists, a vision reminiscent of Def Poetry Jam's transformative power. From the loss of loved ones to honoring his father in a special way, Kwame Mintah's life is a testament to the belief that a greater purpose guides us and we must surrender to it with love.

As you delve into his work, remember the man behind the verses, whose journey embodies the unwavering faith that there's a destiny far greater than one can fathom. Kwame Mintah creates not just from passion but from a profound understanding that his purpose is intertwined with uplifting others.

My early memories of living in West Africa takes place on a refugee camp in Ghana. There, I lived with my mother and siblings. She loves to tell me stories of how even as a toddler, would never come back to her empty handed when I returned from playing with my cousins. "You would always find something to bring back; from a rock to some flowers, you picked."

Fully Loved

4 You

I write this for you;
it has always been about you.
Out of all people, how come I came across you?
You're my favorite coincidence.
No, we prayed for this.
Listen, I'll tell you what you are to me:
a blessing, multifaceted.
Fasten my seatbelt, wide grinning,
I'll take this ride with you.
It's more important to me that I see you winning.
My situation was a win-lose before we met.
A loss because I lived reclusively, a loner.
I had no one to call my own.
A win, cause God knew you were on the horizon for me.
So here it is again, I write this for you.
Honestly, it's all been about you.

I Study You

When I first met you,
I knew it would always be you;
through whatever life throws.
And if I ever lose this feeling,
please replace it with an even better one.
You feel deeply and it's clear
many don't understand that.
But you understand yourself.
I study you.
Let me show you my understanding
through these actions, not words.
Let these nouns become verbs.

Tell Her Again

her favorite compliments are from me;
meaning, the only accepted gestures
are the ones that make her soul smile.
my goal is to allow you
to fully be in your feminine energy;
her safety takes precedence.
i study your expression in the way
you move with the flow of life.
my gift is to innately translate the feelings;
of your lips on mine,
or how i forged a union with your soul.
shea butter in beauty, it's unmistakable;
God crafted you with care.
these words aren't only 4 your eyes & ears;
she needs something she can feel.
i need that, 'i love you from
the depths of my soul' type love.
if i tell her again, i hope she hears me.
if i show her again, i pray she feels it.

Love Again

What do lovers gain?
A question for the heart—you will love again.
And although we're not perfect,
your effort and consistency
are things that make this worth it.
I find strength in my feelings for you.
You are the catalyst.
You have the kind of love
that asks for *nothing*,
but gives you *everything*.
What do lovers gain?
My heart's answer is 'Everything.'
You will love,
Again.

Temptations vs. Desires (pt.1)

I believe desires come with intuition.
Desires may show a clearer path.
Temptations may be temporary
satisfactions and more hazy roads.
Fuck, I need you to care.
Care where I'm at when
I don't show within the hour quoted.
Temptations can be fueled by negative vices.
Desires can be inspired and ignited from the soul.
This soul still wants you.
I'm not tempted to call you,
I desire to hear your soft voice.
I'm tempted to travel at the speed of sound,
I desire to feel your glow, golden brown.

Real Life

I don't need to prove my happiness
with you on social media.
We do this in real life.
That's what really matters.
We're not an Instagram couple.
Just a couple with an understanding
that communication is vital.
(The emotional)
Do you know how rare you are?
I taste these words before I serve em;
My honey, I'm only tryna sweeten up your days.
In real life.

But I'll Admit It

The moral to the story is
A woman needs love.
Not the type that fades
When she's yours.
These words help
My wounds heal.
It helps me unwind
After a period
Of tension.
You cross my mind
A thousand times.
I wanna laugh with you.
Maybe I'm selfish.
But I'll admit it.

I'm Crazy About You

I'm crazy about you.
Like, how I can't miss your calls
because I don't want it to be your last
and I never get a chance to tell you
that I love you again.
It may just be my PTSD kicking in,
I want to make sure you're alright.
all the time.
Like, did you get home safe?
Such a relief every day.
Sometimes, my words may not touch you
the way they should, but I want you
to know that my intentions
have always been true.
So yes, I'm crazy for you,
I'm still crazy about you.

About You

It's about you like it's always been.
Every time I pick up my pen.
I draw from memories,
you would've thought I was painting.
I know it's you.
You know it's real
when even *the silence feels loud*.
I grab hold of you,
with the same grip
that I *hold my dreams with*.
This is how I feel *about you*.

Value

If they say that nothing lasts,
you'll be euphoric moments of the past.
You deserve someone
who understands that it takes work;
to maintain, to put in the effort
that it takes to stay in love.
I know that everything takes time.
See, I'm the type to go harder
when I have you as opposed
to lessen value when you're mine.

Down

Don't let the lows get you too down.
Don't let the highs get you too lifted.
Her dream is to ride in a hot air balloon.
Same place I promised myself
I'd get down on one knee.
You look like my girl,
I sound like I've said it before.
This requires trust.
Trust I barely had in myself.
If we elevate with faith,
I don't wanna feel the bottom.
Don't let the lows get you too down.
And don't let the highs get you too lifted.

Only U

They could say you're crazy—no, you're not crazy enough. You're a queen, even if you don't have a king by your side. You could make love to places in my heart that others were too timid to look at. You listen to me, and I give your heavy heart all the love and light my soul can summon. I can't seem to find the words to tell you truly how beautiful you are. Your brown glow is simply magic. I want you to know that you have the fire inside of you that could make hell jealous. Smoky love, I hope that you breathe better when I clear the air, to tell you all that you deserve. I write this message in hopes that every word could serve *only u*.

Imprecise Words

If he wants you—
if a man wants you,
he will show you just that.
He'll turn words and thoughts into actions.
There's something bout the way you know me.
If you ever see her again, tell her that I'm sorry.

Worth the Chase

Yes, I chased you.
Yes, I'm thankful that you
gave me a chance to catch up.

Now it's my duty to show you
that I'm not here to slow you down.

Continue with your pace,
I just wish to be by your side.
I can't guarantee that the sun will stay out,
but if the rain falls, I'll shield you from it.
Functions of an umbrella,
I use these words like the armor they are.

You just need a dry place to be warm,
where you can be yourself.
I wrap my arms around you when I tell you,
I want you happy, I want you smiling,
I want to hear your laughter.
That alone was worth the chase.

Well, I think you kind of Fly

You match my style,
well, I think you kind of fly.

I love the way your fits compliment the magic of your skin
tone. You know your power, girl you do something to me.
Your aura glows, luminously captured my attention.
Like the ways of a moth, I'm attracted to your light.

Maybe it's the beauty...
I love you cause you love yourself.
Under the sun when you smile,
I love the creases under your eyes.
I love your energy,
I love when you're around.
I hate the goodbyes.

You match my style,
well, I think you kind of fly.

Fuck it, I Miss You

Fuck it, I miss you.
And I'm not the type to say that for nothing,
cause I haven't said it in a while.

There's something regal about you.
Your smile – no, your attitude.
What makes you special is that
you're unapologetically *you*.
Devine with all the moves you make.
I cannot fit the essence that shapes you into a poem.
Simply intangible. Yet, I feel it in my soul.

But... she's not easily impressed.
You don't even gotta fuck wit the poetry;
just want you to notice me.
No, I want you to know it's me.
Fuck it, I miss you.

Garden

Now I don't say this to discourage you,
but I'd be remiss if I missed a chance
to reiterate that Roses have thorns.
Like you, they're delicate and protective.
Of what crosses the mind. Their peace.
You're like a Sunflower, you come in a variety,
but there's only one you.
Purple, orange, red, or even a mix of these hues.
You aren't just one flower like you appear; you
embody thousands of smaller flowers.
A ray floret is each pedal you portray.
I promise I am not a botanist. but I study you.
I'll do my best to water your mind and feed your soul.
I wanna treat you like a garden.
Time and attention is important.
It's essential because
I want your garden to be enormous.

I Wanna Hear 'em

I love to learn.
Teach me things.
I don't want to leave this
relationship the same way I came in.
I wanna learn something new about you every day.
Maybe something about the world and its complexities.
I don't want to leave at all.
Can we water each other's minds?
Can we make time?
Can we share our joys?
Can we help to heal from our sorrows? Our woes;
Can you be at peace with no foes?
If I told you I wouldn't bend the rules,
would you believe I'll never fold?
Can we address the things we think are foul?
Can we write down our vows and read 'em out loud?
I wanna hear 'em.

That Look

That look, that look will raise body temperature.
That look, could provide moisture in a desert.
That look, that look will send a tingle up your spine.
That look, that look will have you screaming unwind.
That look, I look to see it every time.

Reciprocity

we have a rhythm that flows when we exchange even energy. i feel a sense of validation in choosing you over every other option. it reaffirms our mutual investment in what we have. no, we ain't keeping score; i just want that mutual love. i just wanna feel safe in the space and depth of the feelings we share. i want a healthy give and take on our way to that agape love.

Poetry Night

can we meet at poetry night if i'm the poet?
could i be your friend b4 your man?
i promise to truly show it.
only God could know your true beauty
embodies the scars you overcame;
i know your heart's pure.
you gotta show this woman that you care about her.
not the, "i mean if she wit it i'm wit it."
i mean the "i gotta make you mine."
Lord knows in each day i'll put in the time.
i'll put in the work; i'll love you so hard
you'll get anesthesia from past hurt.

Vulnerability

Have I ever purposely not
Answered when you call
At any hour of the day?
Why would I start now?
Time and consistency
Are essential.
I get sad and lonely.
Am I being vulnerable with these words?
No, that's not enough.
Saying that you're sad
And opening up a bit is not
All that vulnerability entails.
True vulnerability is having the ability to give
Someone the power to completely
Tear you apart and having to
Trust that they won't.

Granted

With you, I met something
I would want forever.
My words are confessions,
And you're at the center of 'em.
How could I undermine the kind
Of joy and sheer happiness, I share with you?
I say light words with a heavy heart.
I say this; I don't take this for granted.
Feels like my wishes were *granted*.

Hussle & Boog (pt. 3)

Sayin some player shit to
A girl I always wanted.
How long I plotted,
Now how could I ever Front on this?
I know that you're Precious.
I say our name with the same
Texture as I say my prayers.
And you're in them.
Not just praying for us,
I pray for you.
I wanna see you be the
Best woman you can be.
I want you to have the
Happiness that causes
Amnesia for past hurt.

Spill

I could go on and on,
spill my soul out for you.
This is everlasting.
What I feel for you isn't goin anywhere.
We should have a getaway, with a beach.
Somewhere you can get that golden brown tan.
Somewhere you can let go of what doesn't serve you.

Flight 99

I just wanna vibe witchu, fuck a title.
No rivals when I'm with you;
It's just us—*spiritually inclined.*
I pray that our friendship
remains vibrant.
Your abundance of love
and care make it safe for me
to be vulnerable:
You chose me,
And that I cannot overlook.
I'm thankful to be a confidant.

Something Real

Don't let the lust interrupt something real—damn.
I only write when I can't look you in the eyes,
I love to daze deeply.
You know how beautiful you are but,
you are graceful.
I'm grateful to have met you.
I wanna balance you out,
I wanna be the one you can confide in.
I wanna be your friend even when I don't admit it.
You are the type to give the world the real you.
You wear your heart up on your sleeve.
I hate it when you leave.
This is something real.

Warmth

I care too deeply.
I feel too much.
That light tint in your
Eyes are always calling my bluff.
You know I like you,
Especially when I deny it.
It's something special that you do to me.
You are my sun when the rain pours
enough for a swim:
I wanna feel the warmth of your skin.
And if I'm seen with anyone,
I'm proud that it's a *Black Queen.*

That's Real

If I ever complimented the way
those brown eyes melt into golden rays in the sun,
it's because I feel a connection to your soul—*your window.*
You let the light within shine through and it's truly radiant;
these are the moments I want to last forever.
When all is said and done, your arms
are where I still find comfort.
That's real.

I Got U

She thinks to herself,
'how would they respond
when I say I miss him?'

Child please,
That's on them

None of your concerns.
Miss him as you please.

She gives love freely.
Her touch is soothing
like wind against grass.

I pray it lasts.

I'm here for you.
If nobody got you,

I got you.

I Got U II

Her touch remains the
Most soothing sensation.
Whatever you do,
Don't let go of my heart.
I want to stay longer with you.
Beauty like the love
I feel radiating within you.
More than a lover,
A friend through thick n' thin.
If nobody got you, I got you.

All Of a Sudden

All of a sudden,
these words become about you.
The sun shines bright on you—it is perfect,
so perfect that it rivals
what I see when you smile.
Your lips hold enough words
and dialects for you to be understood.
I wanna tell you that you are enough
and you've always been.
I wanna, not only make songs and write poems about you,
but make you playlists and send you books.
You know, feed your soul and water your mind.
What I'm really asking is for you to *be mine*.
And all of a sudden,
these words become about you.

I Wanna Talk to You

(Phrase) Let me reassure that this soul still wants you.
I wanna go at your pace, though this heart gets filled with a
rush of inspiration; or ambition to make you mine. I'm not
tempted to call you; I desire to hear your soft voice. I'm not
tempted to travel at the speed of sound, I desire to feel your
glow, golden brown.

Cold Feet

This morning was a rainy one.
So, I called you for some sunshine.
Have you ever felt your soul smile?
Have you ever felt happiness
In the midst of dark moments?
Few moments pass where
I don't complicate if I should show you what you deserve.
My appreciation runs deep.
You the type to make a brotha get cold feet.

I Know the Real Thing

You gotta let me hold you, cause you're the one
I wanna be with… Tears have no fear when I'm here for
you. Here I go again; speaking to her, I can't distort the
thoughts. I love these memories. Even when it gets lost, the
flavors in the feelings find its way, still. Just caught in deep
pondering, pay me no mind. Attracted to the way you pay
attention, you listen. Drawn to the power that you stand in.
Some may be intimidated. Some even try to emulate it.

I know the real thing.

Love Language (pt.1)

Let's be real—gifts and surprises are my love language.

Though I speak a few other dialects
that are just as beautiful.
Like, good communication.
Listening to come to an understanding,
not to be right or wrong.
I could shower you with gifts and flowers,
but what happens when my actions sway
when the roses fade?
I'm tryna be fluent in how you're feeling.
Not simply filling you up.
There's power in knowing that you
can speak exactly what's on your mind.
And I cherish that; never wanna be the reason that subsides.
Studying your vocabulary so I
can better comprehend the intense novel that is you.
Cause it's the little things that count the most.
Channeling these nouns and verbs
into reality so you can feel it close.

Let's be real—gifts and surprises are my love language.

Destiny

This one is for good measure.
I'd be lying if I said I wasn't mesmerized.
Not even by your thighs,
I wanna gaze deeper in your eyes.
I wanna tell you personally.
Instead, I put it into words.
One thing you couldn't curve.
Drawn to the femme fatale.
I get puzzled by the lack of response.
I want a piece of you to complete this picture.
(The Emotional)
It doesn't matter if I've written this in vain.

Too Rare Otherwise

I don't wanna write this down,
I wanna speak from the heart.
But here I go again, things fall apart.
You got me.
I just can't keep calling her, home.
So just let me be lonely tonight.
I've grown accustomed.
You're not perfect, you're custom.
One of one. I could search my whole life,
Them girls ain't as regal as you.
I wanna to be wrapped in your arms.
I don't wanna worry much.
I think it's time to love on you.
These smiles hit different when I think of you.
So do you love her now?
Did you ever love me, though?
She's too rare otherwise.

Intrinsic Magic

You're the first person
I call when I'm finished writing.
Kind thoughts revolve around my mind
through these pieces.
I ain't lying; I mean I once was.
We all have. But you seem like good vibrations.
You are relaxation in my tired search for comfort.
Intrinsically speaking, I think you're magic.
I think love is *Intrinsic Magic* in the universe.
And your glow evinces that you're a star in human form.

Sincere

I speak sincere.
I don't need a muse,
I just need you to exist.
She said I was impatient.
I looked up ways to be more present.
Her love is rare,
My heart is light.
I wanna speak my heart,
I wanna tell you that I love you.
I speak sincere.

I Wanna Hear 'em

I love to learn.

Teach me something, please.
I don't want to leave this relationship
the same way I came in.
I wanna learn something new about you every day.
Maybe something about the world and its complexities.

I don't want to leave at all.
Can we water each other's minds?
Can we make time?
Can we share our joys?
Can we help to heal from our sorrows?
Our woes,
Can you be at peace with no foes?
If I told you I wouldn't bend the rules,
would you believe I'll never fold?

Can we address the things we think are foul?
Can we write down our vows and read 'em out loud?
I wanna hear 'em.

Simplicity is Key

I don't want to be madly in love.
I want to love, sanely and happily.
Cause I care for the simple things.
I want us to share our joy,
not to depend on one another
to bring each other that.
I believe that's part of
what it's about—
Simplicity.

Count Your Blessings (pt. 1)

The day I met you, I met eternity.
In a sense—I just knew you'd
be a part of my existence forever.

Chemistry has done more for me than biology.
Vibe intuition has told me more truths than words.
Cause the right vibes can feel like magic.
Like a piece of a puzzle, filled.

Before I let you walk away,
I'll risk being fired for asking you to stay.
Stay an extra 15 seconds.
Your digits are only 10— to the number I could call.
I was on cloud 9. *I counted the blessings.*

Every small gesture following
that moment held the most space in my heart.
Reality only crept at the moments that we were apart.

Years For

She is the only woman
who I would wait years for.

I'm telling you,
she is regal in all that she bears.
Please bear with me as
I share my heart with you.

She's not perfect, but she is pure
with her intentions and kind to her core.

Outer beauty is attractive,
but what's inside is a soul of gold.

She is the only woman
who I would wait years for.

You're Too Precious

I kill every trace of my ego when
I write, so you know it's from the heart.
Cause if you cease to exist, the universe would
notice. Every moment matters when I'm with you—
I say these words out loud.
I hope you feel it.
I still spill my soul to you;
You're too precious.
I only write these words when I'm in my feelings.
They say there's no money there; I beg to differ.
But you always made your own.
How do you harness the power
to shake up every room you enter?
The kind of power to be true to yourself
and still find a way to grace the covers on Vogue.
Soft and delicate, but don't be confused;
her heart has a gear that switch to cold like Anna Wintour.
You wouldn't dare push it there.

Yana May

Yana May, Yana May.
You're on to me.
I appreciate you.

Can I express my deepest concerns for you?
Can I love you without you wanting me to care a bit less?
I plant these seeds and give it time to watch 'em grow.

When you're in pain, I know your heart won't let it show.
I say that judging from your smile.
Your glow is warm enough for me to feel it in my palm.
Whatever books you're diving into,
I wanna help guide your mind.
I'm not here to make your waters murky.
I pray to the most high over the PH, 9 for the highest
balance of liquids that could water your mind.
Holy water...
Remember *Holy Sunday*?

I'm Aikeem Vill,
I want you to remember me.

Wife Kind

You are the wife kind.
I pursue your presence with 10 toes down,
I wasn't just tryna get my feet wet.
It's obvious that you
were much deeper than many could dive.
I told myself that I'd make you mine.
These dreams, I just can't predict.
But you always told me to plan it till it exists.
You're the reason I made an Exit.
I'm the reason we exited what we had.
Still made sure the door was unlocked.
Even if it wasn't, I never asked you
to return the keys to my apartment.
Honesty, I wanted you to live here.
You always had your own.
A grown woman.
'No, you don't need a loan' woman.
Not even a man to help you financially.
It's no wonder you can't escape my mind.
You are the wife kind.

Chemical Bond

you make chemicals react
throughout my nervous system.
like when i first fell in love with hip-hop.
her aura is more jazz and soft r&b.
i wanna know where
the power of a woman stays.
from now on i wanna stay with you.
i'll speak to you with prayer textures when i lay with you.
how could i go back to just temporary satisfaction
when i've found soul nourishment?
i would give you the world but i can't purchase what
you already possess. her aura is jazz and soft rhythm.
you make chemicals react throughout my nervous system.

Soulful Bliss

I found someone I could write
about til the pen's outta ink,
until my thumbs bleed.
Cause I'm in love with
the way your love feels.
No, not feels, it fills my heart with so much joy.
Euphoric wonders,
where were you all my life I wonder.
I wanna be wrapped up in you.
Wrapped up in all of this,
wrapped up in a *soulful bliss*.

Consistency and Patience

i usually have no trouble opening up, but 4 you i feel i have
to be more cautious. i care because i don't wanna mess up.
though i know i'm not perfect, i want you to see the light
and potential in me. often times in my younger days, i did it
the impatient way. meaning, i would've pursued you with
too much urgency. i had to release my fears of you being
scooped up by another man. i knew what i wanted but not
how to go about it. these days, i balance these words and
actions as you allow it. attracting you with positive
vibrations while picking up on your aura. i wanna know
your wants and needs so i can meet them. still trusting my
own intuition. no unrealistic expectations, just consistency
and patience.

Agape

I want a friendship without egos attached.
I want real selflessness from one another.
I want a place to call home.
I want that connection that you
never question its strength.
I wanna stay attuned to her
needs and problems.
I want that balance created from
an understanding so deep that
it goes unspoken between us.
I wanna motivate you
toward inner growth
and still be a comfortable place to fall.
I want a demonstration of *Agape love*.

Crave

You gotta crave me.
Don't I dream about you enough?
You gotta be ready for me.
I've been preparing my whole life.
You can't be too sensitive, I'm intense.
I've been through the Fire.
What are your intentions?
This peace of mind means the world to me.
To be connected as if you were a piece of me.
Are you sure this could work?
Only actions could answer that.

Crave II

do you love me cause i fear that
i care about you certainly.

**what's the rush,
what's the urgency?**

i want you in my life, soul's on fire;
it's an *emergency.*

boy, don't play wit me...

we too grown for the games.

send me flowers if you fr.

i have something more
beautiful in mind.

beautiful like this mind?

mindful like my actions.

actionable like your plans?

plentiful like abundance found in you.

If It Hurts

I talk to you
Like you are mine.
Wait, wait, wait.
You *are* mine.
And it's like,
I'd give it all to you.
You gotta feel me.
If this works, I'll find you.
And if it hurts, I'll find myself.

Mastermind Partner

having the right woman right beside you on your mission in this world is so crucial… it's not talked about enough but women are what kept most of the people we revere sane. the right woman can really change your life 4 the best.

she will be a *mastermind partner.*

essential

i wrote about her like she needed me.
but i needed her, felt like she
was the piece to complete me.

i have never looked at you
and not seen my woman.

i get *butterflies* on the back of my *kneecaps*
with every gaze; i can't take my eyes off you.

your very essence is essential.

my yearn 4 you conveys in the existential.

taste

once you get a taste of her love,
you'll never settle again. you'll know
your worth… and hers simultaneously.

she feels a lot, but don't say much.
i'm always a little better when
i'm reminded of your existence.

she replied, *"you really know
how to make a girl smile."*

i just want a woman i can build a life with.

smile

i've been attracted 2 you like no other woman
i've come across on here; you're constantly
wondering why & sometimes downplay it.

my attraction is personified like it's beckoning
me to explore all of your complexities.
i'm simply intrigued and wonder why i'm so
drawn to how your eyes get you *smile.*

music soulmate

you're a melody worth vibing to.

like a song hidden in my heart.
your glow shows me what the sun could do.
your energy emanates what God has done.

we rock with harmony in the physical; in unison
with every tempo. i become invisible, you hit a solo.
My eyes closes as my soul listens. these words and music
go hand and hand. the sound of your heartbeat could
fill the air. i used to want you solely in visuals 4 poetry,
now i want you in my life. i'll treat you like a flower;
i wanna meet you where you're at. i want to water your
mind and nurture you on a spiritual level.
let's pour on to one another. teach me things
in a tone reminiscent of soft rhythm and blues.

Virtue

life is teaching me the true virtue of patience.
patience in how bad i want you and me to be one.
with you, i'd feel like i've won; in all aspects, in
every way it's you i crave. i want my moments
with you to feel like home. in that home, i need
our connection to be the base to our foundation.

i want our principles to lie in communication and
respect, even when we disagree. i wanna hear your
thoughts and feels your emotions. i want you to
know that it's okay to be patient with yourself.
i need your self-worth to be worthwhile.

Top-tier

i know her taste is top-tier
i wanna know if she taste top-tier
i want our connection to not stop there.
i got fiery desires 4 you.
i got soft words and subsequent actions
that are manifested in prayer textures.
i wanna feel you. i want pure intimacy;
the one where i'm solely craving your presence.

She Replied

she asked if i use these lines
on every pretty girl i meet.

babygirl, i just wanna be in love.

i too, wanna be in love
with a beautiful mind.
love crushes me yet somehow
heals me in the same breath.

i'm terrified of the pain, but i don't
know how to hold back.
i desire more than a soulmate;
i need a twin flame.
fiery desires are in my soul 4 you.

diamonds

i've been meaning to say
this for some time now:

*i want everything
to do with you.*

i'm just tryna make sure
that ring on your finger
sparkles a bit more.

cause my soul interacts
with your light in ways
that are parallel to how light
interacts with *diamonds.*

Intimacy

I want you to lay on me; it's intimacy I want.
I want your touch. I want you to look me in my eyes and
smile. Laugh with me, I wanna feel safe. I want to feel like
you really got me. I enjoy the simple things. I want that
kind, peaceful love. I know your vibration changes as you
refine your higher being. Being with you fructify my soul
and elevates my mind. I meet a deeper version of your
higher self every time we have intense conversations.
You hear every word my spirit spill, you're my
congregation. Your love helps me grow my wings so that
I can rise above all the pit falls. You help me balance it all.
I give this weight called love all back in return.

Find her love

Holy water & hellfire,

To find her love I'd
travel every meter.
Her soul reaction
depends on how I her treat her.
I *want* her.
I don't need a girl,
I need a *woman*
who's my life partner.

I wanna bring you flowers and take you
somewhere with cloth napkins and lights
from fire candles; I wanna keep you warm.

I wanna add value to your existence.

the source

why does she have my pen flowing
so effortlessly? is it weird that
i think she knows how i feel...

you're a work of art, therefore
i articulate matters of the heart.

but ***she's the source*** and she gets
it from a ***Higher source;*** allowing
her to show up as her ***highest self.***

*i'm ready 4 you; in every
way that i can imagine.*

Loyal

i realized that i'm lookin 4 a genuine friend,
someone who i can call a life partner above all else.

she makes feelings of things being missing disappear.

i'm completely loyal to you; love me unconditionally.
may these life challenges become less of an issue with u.
my goal is the help you feel whole, reciprocity on full.
simplify my life, see being with you feels like relaxation.

Reassurance

She's like medicine 4 the soul.
Therefore, I'm so invested.

I know that reassurance is key.
She knows she has the key to my heart.

I never hid it, not even from the start.

In a poem (WYD?)

I barely text but,
I gotta make sure you're
The top thread so,
WYD?
She replied,
"Redefining my purpose."
My response,
"You're a part of
What makes the world better."
I feel your search in my soul.
I rather be spending time with you
Than laying at home alone.

I can find you

I know that things take time to become something
beautiful. I value your authenticity, in a world full of lies.
I'm blessed just to lie here with you. I could find you, even
in the dark. Cause you're all I've been looking for. If I let
my heart guide, you'd be all that see. Adore me. From
close distances or even miles apart. I feel you softly like
flower pedals, I speak to you with prayer textures…
I could find you even when I'm in the dark.

I wanna talk to you

If I talk to you,
I feel I will be filled
with a rush of inspiration,
or ambition to make you mine.

I wrote sober but spoke to her
slightly less than the most high.

I value her time and space.

Only time she trips is when she
touchdown from the stars.

Sometimes I gaze at
them and I think of you.

Connection

I don't wanna lose this connection.

I just want that feeling back;
that feeling that I won't take for granted.

We are emotional beings and indeed, we need company.
You're already occupying a great deal of space in mind.

I feel silent wars of the heart.
There is power in your softness,
there's a fire inside you.
One that could be used as a light.
One that laminate my world.

My soul lights up when we're together…
And when we're apart, call me when you're home.
We're flowing, not attached.

I don't wanna lose this connection.

I want you in my life

You look like my girl.
I sound like I've said it before.

I want you on my feed daily.
She's a walking aesthetic.
Poetry without words.
I want you in real life.

Ethereal being,
She gets it from the source.

A source of pure joy.
She leaves me feeling
Weak in the knees yet still,
She's a source of strength.

I find magic in these words and
Slowed down to see what I truly needed.

All because I want you in my life.

Tell

She's my girl, but she's not my girl.
We simply smile and light up
when we get together.
I just like talking to her.
I love your company;
I'm not lonely.
I mean, only on the inside.
I still wanna know you inside out.
I care about you like you're mine.
I still wanna make you mine.
It's love… Love that I feel.
These words aren't about you.
Stories I tell you when I try to conceal
how much I pour my heart in your well.
I think I met you for a reason,
only time will *Tell*.

Tell II (stuck on you)

At what point do I just tell you
that I love you?

Straight up.

I want you
and everything to do with you.

I'll tell you again,
I choose you.

Your aura is magnetic.

I'm left with no choice but
to run in your direction.

Stuck on you.

I make the time cause I love you.
Cause when you love someone,
You *don't* make excuses.

Universal Cues

Let's rekindle what we
Had and find what we lost.

We may have needed more time.

But that's a figment of imagination,
I imagine it was communication
That needed configuration.

Plus you're a Pisces,
Not easily predicted.
Therefore, *I study you*.

Someone I wasn't looking for
But the one I needed the most.

Universal cues.

I listen to the signs like I listen to you.

Masterpiece

It's what I love
Most about you.

You dive for your dreams,

Unabashedly.

Reached for the stars,
Your *Inner Work* has
Made you a masterpiece.

It's about us

We can make this
Work if we tried.

It's about us.

How could you know
What love is if you don't
Even know who you are?

There's a lot that I
don't know but still love.

Like all the passion you have.

Some say you're crazy.
No, you're not crazy enough.
You're a queen, even if you
Didn't have a king by your side.

You could make love
To places in my heart that
Others were too timid to look.

I know that we
Can make this work if we tried.

It's about us.

Still I

I wanna hold your
Hands because
We're stronger together.

The vibe feels more than
Words when I open up.

Deep breath,

Lord knows you're
Something beautiful.
Would you reach for a
Light if you saw me
In the dark?

Are these emotions
True or am I playin'
With my heart?

Still I, wanna hold your
Hands because
We're stronger together.

Down to Mars

That girl is no good for me.

But I really think she's down to Mars.

We just be fightin' these feelings.
Feeling like I'm still fightin' for you.

I know that you're deserving of love,
Just as you are. You're doing enough.
It's not required to push to full capacity.

Your existence is enough for me.
But I really think she's down to Mars.

You (I wanna talk about her prelude)

Every girl just can't be you.
They wouldn't even know how.

This shit is rare.

It wasn't by accident,
We collided for a reason.
I still believe this deeply.

I Wanna Talk About Her

I wanna talk about her! I'm fired up.
I recall those feelings; these were real feelings.
They were honest feelings.
Like, the only girl my heart desires.
Like, the person I think about
throughout the day feelings.
Like, I wish you were mine feelings.
Like, you're gorgeous—period,
Not "for a dark-skinned girl" feelings.
Like, let's have gorgeous dark-skinned children feelings.
Like, we're still in high school
and you're new here so I must act now feelings.
Like, the best memory of my life is when I kissed you
in my environmental science class after lunch feelings.
Like, I can go on and on because
I still want you in my life feelings.

U Nasty

You nasty and all dat.
I'm talking the fun that
encompasses way more.

You mean wit it.
I'm talking bout you
saying what you said.

I'm just not tryna lose you.

Whatever we do,
Let's promise to have fun.
And promise to smile through.
Never take ourselves too serious.

Long as I keep my word.
Long as they know I'm yours.

Things I Wanna Tell You

Everyone doesn't
Deserve you.
Sometimes, I think
It includes me.

I live in an
Ocean of emotions.
You fluidly drift
Through my thoughts.

Things I wanna tell you:

Emotionally and
Intellectually remain
In your vibration.

You are the frequency of
The good that I desire.

Peninsula

Life can get easier.
Things can be beautiful.

Life gets hard sometimes,
but I hate to see her frowning.

I hate to see her frownin'.
I hate to see her frownin'.

"The emotional"
No. Because I care.

How do I life your spirits?
My soul feels compelled.

Long as I don't ever feel
impelled to ask you
questions like,

Do you love me?
Is this special for you?

Fully Loved (pt. 2)

If you think I love you,
Just know it's true.

You deserve to be Loved, Fully.

I know the pain shaped you
Into an experienced fighter.
You've walked through hell,
You've experienced fire.

I wanna give you what you
Deserve while you still care.
You deserve someone who knows
Your value while you're still there.

Someone who believes what you
Say and acts accordingly.
And is secure enough to know you
chose them out of countless other options.

I care for you, *Fully*.
I feel so much in hopes
That you feel it too.
I never said goodbye
So I'll always wait for you.

You deserve to be Loved, Fully.

Fully Loved

We can go back and forth.
But one thing that's not up for
debate is how much love I'll give you.

You deserve to be loved, fully.

You see, people are like flowers.
What you put in, more often than not, is what you get out.
All she ever asked for was some time and attention;
someone who would listen.
I'm invested, my heart's been rooted in you.

So may I, *water* your mind and *nurture* your soul?
Show you what it means to be loved, fully?

Compelled

It's Kwame

I can do some things,
I just want them to be worth it.
Some days, I feel worthless.
We all struggle with hard times.
It's the human experience.
Experiences with you are some
of my favorite parts of this journey called life.

Wishing you were my wife.
Wishing you well, in general—
generally speaking, I love you.

I use these words like a shovel,
it helps dig me out of my lowest points.
These thoughts are poignant.
Wish I could borrow the essence
of the shine within you.

Prolific

As I speak, I create.

Words are powerful, and I understand the meanings.
They're not all about you, only the overwhelming majority
of them. Aware of what I say and how I say it; these words
have power to direct fate. To pick you up when you're
down, or even turn your life upside down. You know me
inside-out, but every day, we learn something new.
I'm learning that my heart still lies with you.

Grateful

I came to the world in a house covered with bullet holes.
If this message doesn't take off, I want whoever reads
this to know that gratitude is a must. I am grateful.
Grateful to God for it all. The good, the bad, the ups and the
downs. I'm at a point in my life where I've experienced
some of the worst things imaginable, but yet, I've found
a way to make it through. I know that things will work
out in the end. Your mind dictates a lot, why keep it heavy?
Say what's on your heart and appreciate everything.
Take a lesson from it all and grow.
These scars have become stripes of strength.

Body

My body.
I spent too long trying to convey
the connection between that and my confidence.
Time led me astray from my old ways.
Ways of high self-esteem.
See, I might've only gained a few pounds,
but the stretch changes to the skin felt heavy.
It lays heavy on my heart that I let the way my
shirt fit dim my shine in this dark world.
No, this isn't who I wanna be.
But I love myself for my inner self.
The only real concern is good health.
Joy and happiness, and surely you've
acquired true wealth.
Don't change a thing about you.
But be a better you.
Love yourself better.
Tend to your needs more.
Rest when you need it.
Ease into complete stops.
Don't let this world dim your
shine ever again.

Ache

My heart breaks every day.
I wish it didn't.
I wish that my pain didn't weigh as heavy.
I wish I could have achieved my goals a lot sooner.
 I wish I would achieve my goals right this moment.
Allow me to take a moment to think it through.
Thinking about you.
Again, it's very common.
You are uncommon.
Trust and honesty isn't common.
You were that.
At least the parts that mattered.
We liked to vibe mostly.
She liked a little liquor in her system.
I just wanna pour my heart out to you.

Every Poet

Every poet just
Wants to be loved.
I'm not a monopoly.
And I don't mean to be
Complicated, I just
Know I can't replace you.
It's like your presence
Has impacted me deeply.
Beyond belief.
You wanna feel
Safe with me.
Training my heart
to be as beautiful
As these words.
Cause I know that deep
Down inside, every poet
Just wants to be loved.

Untitled

Doing all the right things
for the wrong people.

But if I do it for my-self
they tend to add an *"ish"*
to the end of the word.

I've had experiences that
has made me feel like end
of the world. I even jumped
out of character, out of
my head, out of my mind.

Karma age like wine
so be kind to her.

How Will You Breathe?

Do you need me
Like I need you?
Forgiveness is key.
I'm talking forgiveness of self too.
Who could love you
Better than you?
Healing starts within,
Transformative healing
Doesn't take a day,
Or a month, or even a year.
There is no set time
For your journey
To living your fullest life.
The goal is to have
The courage to begin,
And stick it through.
Your happiness matters.
Cause if you don't
Get it off your chest,
How will you breathe?

I Know Me

God knows me.

I found peace for the first time in a long
time when I asked to be used by You.
Committed to my own growth.
I've chosen to choose myself again.

My peace is untouchable.

You know, love myself endlessly.
I'm breathing better.
Things have not been easy,
but I need me. And I'm still here.
All that exist is the present
moment, and I cherish
these precious memories.

*I know me
and I'm good.*

Care 4 Me

Exhaustion weighs on my body
Each day, but escapes the lull of rest.
Exhausted from it all.
From the amount of effort,
From the pressure,
From societal beat downs.
Want me to make beats now?
Can't you hear my heart drum?
I feel like I'm tryna do the impossible
With no assistance.
Disappointment is felt within.
From old habits I try to shake.
Living in a slumber when I'm awake.
I fell asleep—like no bed,
sleeping on myself and my highest vibration.
Do you care for me?
Care for me.
Care 4 me.

All That Needs to Be Said

How will you reach your destination
when you have God in the back seat?
Sit, recline your seat and think about it.
I say it and weep.

Solid

I don't want to be
the world's most thorough man.
I just want to be
solid enough where I stand.
A concept I've been
desperately tryna land.
With interest from the same label
heads who released "This Plane."
Still not as fly as Yana.
Intuition saying, 'stay in your lane'.
I'm not into wishin.
I'm not into letting
what I want get away.

Self-Love

If you were wondering where I've been,
I've been on a deep search for the love within.
That mind over matter love for self.
That, "I won't be ashamed of the battles
my spirit fought for survival" love.
I know that we needed space.
I grasp that *space and solitude*
can act like oxygen for us to heal.
If you were wondering where I've been,
I've been on a deep search for the love within.

No More

I don't want to pour
Out the light of my Inner-Sun
If I'm not your sky.
But we are our own sun.
I'm brave, so I still love.
You're the type I broke
Some of my own rules for.
How could I let pride
Get in the way?
I'd be a fool.
Who would've thought
You'd do me foul?
We all can find love,
I just want one that's
True to stay.
No more half-ass
Or fake love.

Breathe

I can breathe easy knowing
That things will work out in my favor.
My intuition is my internal GPS.
Managed by my faith in God,
I trust my direction.
No more looking for
Love in the wrong places.
I've made the decision
To prioritize my inner peace.
That means even forgiving me.
I can breathe easy knowing
That things will work out in my favor.

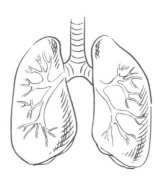

How I'm Doin'

All I do is shed tears.
Tears flood as my emotional
Levee seems to instantly
Collapse at the thoughts
Of my current predicament.
I am hurting.
This isn't a cry for help.
It's a cry for strength from above.
And I've been strong for so long.
I've lived through trauma
I could barely withstand.
But I refuse to let my momma down.
I let it out, but know when to stop.
That's when I wipe the tears from my eyes.

Girls Get Lonely

I know that girls get lonely.
She wants to feel our souls intertwine.
She wants me to wine and dine.
With fine words; food for thought.
But what good is any language
If unfeigned actions are lost?
I know that girls get lonely.
It's not her fault.
Still, I'm lost without your touch.
You're my never-ending thought.

A Mazed

I don't want much. I just want her.
She was there when I needed her the most;
with intimacy as delicate as a gaze.
She's a puzzle, I'm amazed.

Euphoric

I don't want a love that only exists in my head.
I wanna be ahead of all the curveballs that life throws.
I desire the mate of my soul.

(Dis) Comfort

If I had to do it all over again,
I'd still choose you.
This time, I'll have a better version of myself.
She don't judge me, even when I judge me.
At times, I try to wait for when the time's right.
But these words I wanna share with you right now.
No over the phone shit, more I wanna see in my room shit.

Faith in Action

You are God's gift.
I put my Faith in Action.
And fight for things
that truly matter.
You.
And if I'm not in love,
I know that *love is in me.*
I want you here, permanently.
Like my scars that you make feel beautiful.
I yearn for the warmth my heart feels
when I'm at home with you.
You are God's gift.

Tension

I fear that I am playing you too close.
I fear that I will be hurt.
I fear that you don't think the same of me.
I fear that I'm not listening to my intuition again.
I fear that I should.
I fear that I haven't found the one.
I fear that I'm too caught up in your external beauty.
I fear that I get lost in the brown tint in your eyes.
I fear that I hold onto you because I'm lonely inside.
I fear that I'm seeking attention.
I fear that I will ruin this.
I fear these words will cause tension.

Balance

I express my heart with abandonment
of what's holding my mind back.
I just need someone to help me balance this existence.
Is this weight called love or infatuation?
Just being honest, I'm fixated.
I wanna know more about you
without pressuring you.
I wanna be aggressive,
but not possessive.
I wanna be persistent,
but not obsessive.
I need to find a balance.

Growth Is Essential

You held a place
in my heart since we first met.
But I can't place this burden on you.
I needed the strength to walk away.
The *separation can be the oxygen necessary to heal.*
It's necessary to build; build as in mature,
mature as in growth.
And *growth is essential.*

More Free

My heart aches
but my mind is resilient.
I've adapted over time.
An evolution and journey
To my higher self.
I'm not insane to
Lose myself in something
I truly wanted.
I'm not ashamed.
I got drunk and called
You a hundred times.
I even sent a message.
I just hope you read it.
I just hope the readers
feel my soul speak.
And I hope you
never felt *more free.*

Prayer

A thing I've been missing
the most; a connection.
With the two most vital components,
my inner being and the lord above.
What good is it to be aligned and not prayed up?
What good is it to be woke and not spiritual?
My core felt off-balance.
I needed someone who would listen and knows my heart.
See this weight is too heavy for normal strength of man.
I need supernatural intervention. I need the right intentions.
So I pray to you and I say it out loud, I need you.
I ask for forgiveness. I ask you for strength and light
during my darkest moments. I pray for protection
and healing from that which sought to torment.

Prayer II

Some things I've been missing
the most; joy, patience, faith.
Open:

I need to speak my truth
And seek your peace.

I know true joy can be found through Him.
I know that patience is a fruit of the spirit.
I know faith is all I have.

Here is my Prayer II:

I pray that I do right by everyone
I meet; even those who disagree.
I pray I learn to channel inner-peace.
I pray you see my vision isn't solely for my own gain.
I pray to someday spell love without pain. I know these
blessings aren't undermined.
Dates with you
I pray I never miss.
When I spend time with you,
I pray these thought never drift.

Close:
"Be joyful in hope, patient in affliction, faithful in prayer."

-    Romans 12:12

Prayer III

Lord, hold my hands along the way;
I need guidance.
Wrap me with your love;
I need the comfort that only comes from you.
Have mercy on my soul;
I need your grace.
Use me 4 your will; at *your* pace.
It's in your presence that joy is sought.
To find refuge in you is what I've learned.
Soften my heart so I may have
the courage to surrender my concerns.

Prayer IV

i want to walk in your ways always.
please remind me i'm in the world and not of it.
You know what i'm facing, and what i've overcome.
i pray to bring healing with these words.
though at times, i mess up and have to begin again,
i ask that you continue to grow these things —
love, joy, peace, patience, kindness, goodness,
faithfulness, gentleness, and self-control in my life.

Console

Who the hell helps the 'strong friend'
when they need conversations
that leads back to revelations?
Comfort my disappointments.
Do you know what it's like to console me?
To listen to me and hear me out?
I just wanna be felt heard and understood.
Sometimes, I speak to the most high.
Less than I should, I still put this faith in You.
Like the trust she had; know when you're wrong.
I know forgiveness from within
will give the courage and strength to win.
I'm through with all the dark patches,
I know the evils only be inviting more demons.
You stopping yourself. Heal it off—repent.
Console.

Who I Am

Grief can bring you low,
but prayer and faith will
take you high.

I'm talking about all the
hurt and the pain.

She told me
not only men could be Kings.

Spread her wings. She learned
that sometimes, just the feeling
that we gave it our all makes
all the difference.

And there is nothing stronger
than a broken woman who
has rebuilt herself.

Not a persecution of men,
She added.

Just
Who I Am.

Compelled

Have you ever given a motivational speech
while hurting on the inside?
These days, "how are you?" comes off as rhetorical.
I don't wanna answer that; the coldest summer ever.
The worst pain is knowing it's your fault.
I use these words as a combat mechanism
to prevent depressive dives.
Treating lovely memories
like they still appear in front of my eyes.
In actuality, they live in my heart.
I keep them all in my good thoughts.
And I keep you on my good vibes list.
You weren't the poet but your aura was poetic.

You are the Sun

Altered Vibrations

You turn nothing into something,
Cause you're everything.
Attracting everything that is necessary,
You are God's highest form of creation.
Altered vibrations.
Believe that you deserve
All the good that is coming your way.
You make the stars envious of your glow,
The moon jealous of your light.

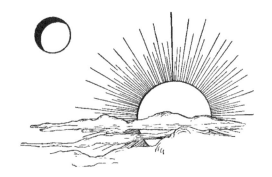

Don't Sleep On You

You are easy to love.
But you don't know that.
It's okay if you changed.
I still give af about redemption.
The world needs you.
I'll still tell you to go
After what you want,
Even if it's a rougher road.
I need to explore this further.
Still curious, erratically
Feel myself drowning in
This life as an Aquarius.
This internal sadness of Sagittarius.
Sensitive; I see more in your potential.
And fu*k 'em if they still sleepin' on you,
Just *don't sleep on you*.

She

She's cold, but known to burn
those who set her soul ablaze.
Delicate, yet fierce.
She is a thinker.
She plans it all out.
She doesn't say much.
She is a mystery.
She's what she says to me.
She tries her hardest.
She feels in abundance.
She doesn't expect much.
She yearns only for time and attention.
She's a breath of fresh air.
She seeks water for her mind.
She's a healer.
She is a blessing.
She is a keeper.
She could use a reminder:
She matters.
She is beautiful and worth loving.

Sun's Flower (She II)

She is like a Sunflower.
She's bold, warm, and exudes a spirit of light.
She comes in a variety; but she is the only one.
If anything, she's everything.
She waters her mind and feeds her soul.
Above all, I hope she knows that
She is of the essence.

Mothers

Mothers, all seem to flow with nature.
Mother Nature seems to flow with you.

I recognize your greatness.
I admire your perseverance.

A parent, you do it all and still find a
way to keep relevance with appearance.

I look at you and I see the realest.
Your presence is experienced,

I feel your spirit.

Follow

I see you,
Healing alone.
You're your own first love.
Be the loyalty you need.
I pray for peace.
Follow your feet,
Follow your soul.

Variations

Confidently start doing
what's best for you.
I hope you find peace within.
And I hope you keep your
thoughts & intentions pure.
Cause pure thoughts can plant gardens.
And tainted minds can burn amazons.

Variations II (No Matter What)

Selfishly become who you want to be.
You have so much light inside of you,
Try not to block it.
Your frequency still carries your truth.
With full belief that failure is not an option.
Knowing that, you will be alright.
No matter what.

Variations III

You are enough.
In and of yourself.
You only look
Inwards for approval.
Your only rival is the soul
You stare at in the mirror.
Complete and whole;
Ever-evolving.
Variations that keep
Shifting and shaping
Your vibrations.
Reformed.
Societal restraints are pushed
aside to give space for your free form.

Variations IV

Great things take time.
Fill your mind with light thoughts.
A Light heart is a more conscious mind.
The power you have is shown in ways
You manifest positivity.
All with gratitude and grace.

Celestial

She is my words, manifested.
Her presence is like her superpower.
There's difficulty in describing our bond.
I recognize her as a *kindred spirit*.

Her Peace

If it must cost her this,
then it's way too expensive.
Out of the budget. Out of mind, out of vision.
Her intuitions are the prevention of collisions.
That career stresses enough,
I'm tryna create a space for you
to come home and be at peace.
And if you're mine, just say so.
I want your mind to feel
the calmness of a pin drop;
you deserve that at least.
Existence has never been easy for a woman.
This life can be wonderful as well as odious.
You can be an extrovert around those who
bring peace in your life.
Who shares a piece of their light
in a way that intertwines
with what illuminates within you.
And what's inside of her are particles
of the stars that adapt to carbon in her womb.

Inner Work

She's doing the inner work,
Lifting her vibrations.
Breaking those generational curses.
I admire your moves.
That knowledge brings power.
That intuition carries your inner light.
The past hurt will not break you.
I see you; healing, evolving,
becoming happier, stepping into *your* power.
We've all done wrong and we've all done right.
Not a suggestion that you're perfect,
More of a not-so-subtle reminder:
your very existence is worth it.
Look in the mirror, I need you
to see what we're blessed with;
Every inch of your alluring smile.
Divine.

I'm Proud of You (Inner Work pt. 2)

I'm proud to see you
Make peace with
Actions implanted in survival.
Cause you're a Survivor to the fullest.
And it's survival of the fittest these days.
That glow shows more when you
Internalize the love formerly sought from others.
Cause you stopped chasing energies
That wasn't meant for you.
But kept your passion, never watered down
For anyone and began respecting your own aura more.
And do what's best for you.
That self-love gon' save you
When you need it the most.
I'm proud of you.

Unsurprisingly

She's not the mushy type.
But she enjoys a lovers' aesthetics.
Though she may be a bit awkward
at times, she's truly herself.
I'm affected by you
in ways you have yet to see.
Unsurprisingly.

Intention

A force of nature, the catalyst.
Your intuition can see through elusive intent.
She moves with intention.
It's enough for me to simply exist in your presence.

Girls Like You

Girls like you.
Take control of a situation.
Girls like you are simultaneously
soft but fire.
Girls like you
I must show off..
To anyone, anyone that'll listen.
Girls like you feels in abundance.
Girls like you don't ask for much.
Just time and attention.

Girls Like You (pt. 2)

Girls like you—
No, women like you.
Women like you are capricious.
You left your mark on me.
The beauty in your
Authenticity is timeless.
And they love the sentiments I write,
4 you; it's always been about you.
The only Pisces I'd give
Every piece of me to.
I know that good women are wild too.
And you don't speak in tongues,
You speak the language of the universe.
I still admire the God in you.

Peace

she's working on herself;
a work in progress
still, accepting her process.
i don't want a piece of you,
i want peace *with* you.
i need peace within myself;
the one that comes from God.
i pray you add to it.
i want us to really
do this; put in genuine effort
when we go through it.

Keep Your Distance

Try to be a better man to her.
Tend to her.
Listen to her.
Actually hear her out.
There is a real point she's
 tryna make behind the volume
in which she's making that point.
If a woman cares for you,
she *really* cares for you.

Is She Real?

I've found a muse,
but she's God's muse.
I speak to God daily.
I know what's in my heart is felt.
I wanna know if she's real.
I wanna know if we share this much
in common or if this is a common mistake.
I don't wanna misalign with her implication.
I don't wanna read between the lines.
I wanna know if she's real.

Borom Sarrett

Her conception of life,
Her philosophy, her stories.
2.Die.4.
To live and stand behind.
To protect without fear
and minimize forlorn tears.
We all need a shoulder to lean on.
Everything.
She is Everything.
She is you.
She is me.
She is Africa.

Muse

A muse is much more
than appearance through photography.
Who are you as a person?
Her character, personality;
How high is your vibration?
Her iridescent eyes are only icing on the cake.
Her radiant soul is a blessing from His gates.
I let these words do the painting
 when *her body's framed.*

Muse II

Much more than appearance
through photography;
it's more *vivid*.

She's a vibe that carries inspiration.

I see her light and it's brilliant.
She is the fuel.
Precise is her *vision*.
Not only does she illuminate,
she *enlightens*.

With a sight less hazy,
I see her hands can ignite
the world within my mind.

Late Bloomer

She's a late bloomer, but
A woman is not a potted plant.
She encompasses the universe.
I need a compass to your heart.
I need you to come back into my world.
Can we walk around the curves of my words?
Can I show you the affection you were deprived of?
The intuition is an internal
GPS to let me know when you arrive.

4 Everything

Everything you
Are looking for is
Already within you.

You still show
Affection even though
You were affected.

The purity of the soul
Is more important
Than the image.

I still believe
it will be you and I.

Let's choose
the life we want,
And run freely
In that direction.

4 Everything.

U've Grown

You've grown a
Lot from it all.

I know the pain makes
The good feel richer.

I know experience is
The greatest teacher.
And the knowledge of
Self-healing is your
Greatest comeback.

Cause you never truly
Fuck over someone
Who was so solid.

This year I've lost,
Won, cried, laughed,
Loved, but didn't fold

Still the focus remains the
Inner Work for what
Tomorrow holds.

But we are our own Sun

Earnest emotions in the phrase.
This is how I came to literature.

Cultivated a love of reading,
Reading you, reading me,
reading the sun, sun and the
seas, birds and the bees.

How could we feel cloudy
when we're our own sun?

If my sun is internal,
I get my source from within.
It's like the voice in
my head, conscience.

Like the stars, our sun;
we can be all the light we
know in our darkest moments.

But we are our own sun.

Acknowledgments

First and foremost, thank you God for carrying the burdens I faced in 2019. Thank you for hearing my cries and surrender. Since late 2019, You have used me for Your will in sharing these words. I'm so grateful for the results you've produced through my work.

All of my day ones supporters; I shed a tear when I reminisce on how far we've come. Thank you from the bottom of my heart for the unwavering love and patience.

Nadia, thank you for helping me put together the website for my pre-orders. Dhayana, thank you for your willingness to help me from the conception to the completion of this book. And to my sister—Nyama, I would do anything for you. Love you to life.

Made in United States
North Haven, CT
20 April 2024

51561628R00104